GU00863712

How To Be
Creative

DEMYSTIFYING THE CREATIVE PROCESS

Neil Pavitt

Cover design: Aldy Akbar
Typesetting: JD Smith

Published by Lightbulb Publishing
All enquiries to neil@thelightbulbidea.com

ISBN 978-1495272011

For Kalya and Harry

CONTENTS

Introduction

Someone recently said to me, "I wish I was creative, but I haven't got a creative bone in my body". It's hard to believe that some people still think 'being creative' is a gift only bestowed on the lucky few. So I decided to write a short book that anyone could pick up and, by the end of it, know where to find their creative bones.

Now, when it comes to finding your creative bones, you'd think that the people most likely to know where to find them would be the inventors, the artists and the deep thinkers among us. That's probably why the most common question at talks by 'creative people' is, "Where do you get your ideas from?" Unfortunately, their most common answer is, "I don't know". This isn't because they want to keep the secret to themselves; they genuinely don't know.

The reason for this is that the most important part of the creative process happens in our unconscious. This is what makes creativity so magical and frustrating in equal measures. You can't guarantee that you'll come up with a great idea; all you can do is create the conditions for creativity to happen. It's like planting a seed in your garden. You just plant it in good soil and make sure it gets plenty of water and sun. There's no point standing over it shouting "GROW, GROW!"

But before you start thinking that you have no control over whether you'll be creative or not, don't worry: help is at hand. There is a process to creativity.

All the great creative people throughout history have used this process. That's not to say that many of them would necessarily be aware they were following a process. You wouldn't have found Newton under an apple tree saying, "Not now, can't you see I'm in the middle of Stage Three?"

There have already been many books written on creativity, but I found that a great deal of them are full of creativity exercises. Now while creativity exercises can be useful, I don't believe they are vital. After all, do you think the creative people you admire, whether artists, writers, scientists or business people, started their days with creativity exercises? Can you imagine Michelangelo dropping by Leonardo Da Vinci's house and asking him what he was working on, to be met with, "I was going to muse on whether there could be some form of sheet with ropes that would help people fall safely through the sky, but first I think I should paint my room blue; it's meant to aid creativity. Perhaps you can help, you're good at painting ceilings."

I believe the most important thing is to truly understand how creativity works. Then instead of spending your time doing creativity exercises you can spend it thinking about some real problem to which you want to find a creative solution. If you want to write a great novel, read a great novel. Don't read a book about how to write a great novel.

I've written this book as a story, so you won't find a précis at the end of each chapter; but I've summarised all five stages of the creative process at the end of the book. I wanted it to be a book you could sit down and read from cover to cover without worrying that you should be making notes. The story is about two brothers, each of whom represents a different side of the brain, and it follows their discussion about the nature of creativity. Even if you don't enjoy it, your brain will. The brain loves a good metaphor.

1

Why Not Me?

"Every child is an artist. The problem is how
to remain an artist once he grows up."

Pablo Picasso

Venn had just got off the phone after a particularly long and boring call. He pushed his chair back and went next door to see what his brother, Hodge, was doing. When he opened the door, he saw Hodge, feet on the desk, looking out of the window.

"Hard at work, I see," said Venn.

"I'm thinking," replied Hodge.

"Oh, is that what you call it?"

Hodge was someone who most people would describe as 'a creative person'. He wrote children's books for a living and had become very successful at it. But with this success came accounts, invoices, contracts, merchandising rights and lots and lots of phone calls. And this is where Venn came in.

Venn and Hodge were twins. But, as the eldest, Venn had always been pushed to be the mature, sensible one. Hodge, on the other hand, had pretty much been allowed to do what he wanted. Seeing them together, you'd think there was ten years' difference between them, not ten minutes.

Venn had taken up a job in a large London accountancy firm, while Hodge had tried to make it as a writer. After receiving endless rejection letters for his novel, he tried his hand at writing for children and became instantly successful. Venn saw his brother's success as an opportunity to escape the corporate world, and he became Hodge's manager/ agent/accountant. He loved working with his brother; he just found it annoying that the more successful his brother's books were, the more stressful his job became.

Venn stood there, looking around his brother's office.

The walls were covered with pictures that Hodge had drawn and strange photos he'd ripped out of magazines. The shelves were covered with all manner of random objects he had picked up on his travels, while the floor was barely visible under piles of books and papers.

Venn's office, on the other hand, was the complete opposite. Any paperwork was put away in filing cabinets, and the only things that covered the walls were spreadsheets and a year planner. He hated the mess in Hodge's office, but he still envied his free-thinking mind.

"Why can't I be creative like you?" he said.

Hodge took his feet off the desk and turned to his brother.

"You can be creative; everyone can be creative. Come and sit down and let's talk about it."

"I've got calls to make," said Venn, with a sigh.

"Forget the calls. Just come and sit down."

Venn walked over to the sofa, which was also covered with what he would term rubbish, but his brother called 'reference material'. He instinctively started to separate the paper from the magazines and stack it in neat piles.

"Just chuck it all on the floor and sit down," said Hodge, eager to start their conversation.

But instead of throwing everything on the floor, Venn just started to sort it more quickly.

"Okay, okay," said Hodge with a sigh. "If you want to be creative, your first challenge is to chuck all that stuff on the floor. Try to ignore your inner accountant and find your inner child."

"I think my inner child grew up a long time ago," said Venn. "I just think that some people are creative and some aren't, and I'm one of the latter."

"That sounds like a challenge," said Hodge, smiling. "I was a bit stuck anyway, so it'll be nice to have something else to focus on. It might be buried pretty deep, but I'm sure that I can help you to find your inner child. You were creative when you were young; you've just had it knocked out of you by spending your adult life in careers where only logical and analytical thinking are rewarded."

"What do you mean, I was creative when I was young?" interrupted Venn.

"Don't you remember you used to say some really creative things. Mum said you once saw an oily puddle with its many colours glinting in the sunlight and you said, 'Look it's a dead rainbow'. Turn that into a line 'The oily puddle glinted in the sunlight like a dead rainbow' and you've got something really poetic. There you go: inner child found. Proof that you have the ability to be creative."

"Nice try, but you're going to have to do better than that to prove I'm creative. When I said that, I wasn't trying to be creative. I said it through a lack of knowledge. I didn't realise that a rainbow wasn't a living thing. Yes, it's sweet and funny, but it's sweet and funny precisely because I wasn't trying to be clever or creative. I was just making what I believed to be a real statement using the limited information I had. Therefore, ipso facto, I wasn't being creative."

"I don't know about ipso, but with you it's definitely about the factos. It's as if you're trying to prove to me that you're not creative, and if you can, you don't have to try any more. Let me have a think of a plan of action overnight and we'll re-convene in the morning."

2

The Rules

"You can't use up creativity.
The more you use, the more you have."

Maya Angelou

The next day, when Venn arrived at the office, he was greeted by the sight of Hodge banging picture hooks into the wall above Venn's desk. As soon as Hodge saw his brother's face, he stopped hammering and started laughing.

"You're more concerned about the damage I'm doing to your wall than what I'm going to hang on these hooks, aren't you?"

Venn said nothing. His brother knew him too well.

"These are reminders of the barriers to being creative," said Hodge.

He then hung a mirror on one hook, a picture of the London Underground map on the second and a framed white sheet of paper on the third.

"Shall I explain their significance?" he asked.

"I feel like I'm back at school."

"Well, that's not a bad place to start, as that's where our natural creativity usually gets knocked out of us. Children start to lose that open-mindedness and their curious view of the world. School seems to be all about what's right or wrong and learning what other people think. Creativity is all about opening up your imagination, trying to do things differently, discovering what you think. There's no right or wrong in creativity. Just because something's always been done one way, doesn't mean that's the way it should always be done. Which leads me to the picture of the tube map.

This map was originally created in 1933 and was the brainchild of Harry Beck, an engineering draughtsman who'd actually been made temporarily redundant by London Underground. When he initially presented the idea, it was rejected for being too radical. But Beck kept pushing, and eventually London Underground printed five hundred copies to test it out. It was a huge hit with the public and they published a first edition of seven hundred thousand. It didn't follow conventional mapping rules because, as Beck said himself, 'If you're going underground, why do you need to bother about geography?' The point I'm trying to make is that it's important to be open to any possibilities. Try not to be judgemental. When you're thinking creatively, it's always important not to confuse knowledge (other people's ideas) with information (the hard facts). The only thing set in stone on a map of the London Underground is the information: the tube lines and all of the stations on them."

Hodge waited for his brother to say something in response, but Venn was just staring into space.

"Have you been listening?" he asked looking hurt."

"I was just thinking about you describing the tube map as the 'brainchild' of Harry Beck. It's interesting that it's the qualities associated with a child that are always used when talking about creativity."

"Eureka!" shouted Hodge.

Venn looked surprised.

"What have you thought of now?" he asked.

"Not what I've thought of," said Hodge, "what you've thought of. I've never noticed that about the word 'brainchild', but you did. You took something, a word that we take for granted and found a fresh way of looking at it. Welcome to the world of creativity."

"Oh, come on, I wasn't being creative, I was just analysing.

That's what I do."

"Yeah, but you looked at something in a different way, something that I'd never seen before. I'm impressed."

"That's still not what I'd call being creative. It's not as if I've come up with a new idea. Anyway, tell me why you want me to gaze into the mirror and look at a blank piece of paper while I'm doing your tax return."

"The blank piece of paper represents the rules you must follow when you're being creative."

"None?"

"Exactly. Don't censor yourself. Be open to anything."

"I thought creative people were meant to fear the blank piece of paper," questioned Venn.

"Well, yeah, it is good to have some rough idea as a starting point before you sit down. If I asked you now to draw a picture of something, you wouldn't start drawing straight away, you'd spend time thinking about what you were going to draw, but if I said, 'draw an elephant', you'd begin immediately. The important thing is to put pen to paper, even if you think that what you're writing or drawing is rubbish. The important thing is to start.

That so-called fear of the blank piece of paper is where the mirror comes in. The greatest enemy to creativity is you. So many people say that they want to write a story, but very few ever get round to it. They're stopped by the excuses they make for themselves: 'My ideas aren't any good', 'I haven't got enough time', 'I haven't got the right environment to be creative in'. You shouldn't expect the first thing you write to be amazing. It's going to take time. Don't let negative thoughts cloud your mind, don't think too much, and just get writing. As you keep working, the light bulb above your head will start to glow and the idea moths will come."

"Idea moths?" said Venn, wincing.

Hodge looked at him and laughed. "Don't you like the thought of idea moths? Would you prefer it if they were idea butterflies? Unfortunately, butterflies aren't attracted to light, so it doesn't work. What is important is your reaction. It's that knee-jerk reaction that could be self-censoring some of your stranger thoughts. And those strange thoughts, given room to breathe, could turn into great ideas."

"So, you're saying don't be too judgemental about what you create and just spend time thinking, then great ideas will come."

"Yeah, basically."

"I don't know, it just seems a bit … woolly."

"Don't worry; the idea moths will eat their way through the woolliness," said Hodge, smiling.

Venn shook his head.

"See, why didn't I think of that? That's creative, that's lateral thinking; that's what I want to do."

"Well, why don't you have a go, then? Spend tomorrow, not in this sterile environment, but in my office, and try to think of an idea for a children's story."

3

Blanksheetofpaperaphobia

"The difficulty lies not so much in developing new
ideas as in escaping from old ones."

John Maynard Keynes

At nine o'clock the next morning, Venn stood in the doorway of his brother's office, surveying the mess. He suppressed the urge to tidy up, sat down at Hodge's desk and switched on his laptop. He stared at the blank document and waited for inspiration. Nothing. The cursor blinked on and off at the top of the page, like an impatient runner jogging on the spot, waiting to be given the go ahead to race across the screen. He looked out of the window for inspiration. Still nothing. "I'll make myself a cup of tea," he thought.

Half an hour later, after getting distracted by the crossword, he was back at the desk. The cursor was getting impatient now. After another five minutes, the screen was still as blank as his mind. "I know," he thought, "I'll check my emails. There may be something important I need to deal with." He opened his inbox, only to be faced with twenty emails from Hodge all saying the same thing: "checking emails is cheating". Annoyed that he'd been caught out, he slammed the laptop shut and swivelled round in the chair to survey his brother's office.

"I can't tidy the room, that's just what Hodge would expect," he thought. "But surely a little bit of alphabetisation action in the bookcase couldn't do any harm." The third book he picked up beginning with 'A' was booby-trapped. It had a post-it note on the front which read, "A stands for Arse; yours should be glued to the chair at the desk". He couldn't believe he'd been caught out again, and went back and sat at Hodge's desk. But after another ten minutes of blankness, he decided to try a change of scene. He picked up a pad of paper and pen and went to sit on the sofa. "Maybe if I'm a bit more relaxed, the ideas will come," he thought, but still … nothing. He started to doodle, and soon his pad was covered with three-dimensional boxes of all different sizes, but no ideas for children's stories. "Perhaps another cup of tea would help," he thought. As he got up, his mobile rang. He was happy to have the distraction, until he saw that it was Hodge calling.

"Yes?" he snapped.

"Not going well, then," replied his brother.

"No."

"I was probably being a bit unfair on you. As I said yesterday, I usually have the beginnings of an idea before I sit down. You need a spark. Why not try looking through some of the children's books on my bookshelf?"

"I don't want to copy someone else's idea," grumbled Venn.

"You're not copying, you're looking for inspiration. Fill your head with lots of different interesting ideas, and before you know it, an idea of your own will just pop up. That's how it works for me, anyway. If that doesn't work, think about when we were kids and what you liked or disliked, what made you happy or sad. If you still can't think of anything, why not call up our cousin Alan and ask his kids what they're into and what stories they like? Just remember not to get stressed and try to think as laterally as you can."

Once he'd put the phone down, Venn picked up a pile of children's books from the shelf, sat down on Hodge's sofa and started reading. He found it really interesting to see the different techniques that the authors used to engage with children. He definitely found it was getting him into the right frame of mind, but he still couldn't think of a good idea for a book. He tried thinking about his and Hodge's childhood, but all he could remember was playing games that Hodge had invented.

He had lots of good memories of his childhood, but nothing that sparked off any ideas for children's books. Finally he gave Alan's kids a ring. Unfortunately, the only thing they wanted to talk about was 'The Bobbleheads', the latest craze from Japan. Venn spent another hour sitting on Hodge's sofa trying to come up with an idea, but still couldn't think of a thing. By 4 o'clock, after spending the whole day trying to be creative, he decided to call it a day. "Whatever Hodge believes, I think I'm just not creative," he thought.

When he went home, he slumped down on the sofa and switched on the TV. There was a programme on with children talking about their pets. One child was talking about how he cried and cried when his goldfish died. Then BANG! It hit him. He had an idea for a book. What amazed him was the buzz of energy he felt when the idea came to him.

He wasn't going to make his story about a goldfish dying. That would be too sad. But he liked the idea of a boy standing over a goldfish bowl and crying so much that the bowl overflowed. Maybe the goldfish would then have to be moved to a bigger container and the boy would then cry over that and make it overflow as well. He hadn't thought yet about why the boy was crying, but he was sure that he'd come up with a reason.

4

Creative Bones

"The world will never starve for want of wonders;
but only for want of wonder."

G.K. Chesterton

The next day, Venn waited excitedly for his brother to come in.

"I've done it!" exclaimed Venn, when Hodge finally walked in.

"You've got an idea for a children's book, that's fantastic. What is it?"

Venn told him the idea. As he did so, Hodge's smile changed to a frown.

"What's wrong? Don't you like it?" said Venn.

"I think it's a great idea, I just think that it's a bit unnatural that the boy is standing over the goldfish bowl when he cries."

Hodge left Venn with his emails and went into his office. But half an hour later he came bounding back in.

"It should be the fish crying, not the boy. That's funny isn't it, a fish crying?"

Hodge thought Venn would be excited by his suggestion, but his brother just glowered and turned back to his computer screen.

"I spend all day trying to think of an idea, then I finally come up with one that I really like and you get all judgemental and say, 'No, you should do it like this'. I thought creativity was all about being open and not judging."

"I wasn't criticising your idea; I think it's great. I was just trying to improve it. That's why a lot of creative people work in teams; they can add to each other's ideas and make them better. But look, it's just a suggestion. You can do it your way if you want."

"No, your way's better. That's what annoys me - once

again you've proved that you're the creative one."

"Come on, it was your initial idea and I just added to it. It was a joint effort. But anyway, what's important is how you felt when you came up with the idea. Did it feel good?"

"Yeah, it did feel good," said Venn. "I felt a real buzz, but now I think it was all a bit fake, as you did the creative bit."

"I keep telling you," said an exasperated Hodge, "it was a joint effort. Also, that was your first attempt at coming up with a children's story. The first story I wrote was rubbish."

"Ah, so you're saying my story's rubbish, then?"

"Give me strength!" Hodge rolled his eyes. "No, I'm not saying that. I'm just trying to say that, like anything, it takes time to get good at it. You've got to put the work in."

"So, if I work at it and I'm not judgemental about my ideas, eventually I'll come up with something great, will I?"

"Yeah, I think so," said Hodge.

"Sorry, but that's not enough for me. I need more substance. I can't believe that the whole creative process can be boiled down to 'don't be judgemental and keep working at it'. I know there's some magic involved, like the moment a great idea just pops into your head. But it's called the creative 'process', so I want to discover what that process is and what the steps are."

"You've just experienced it," sighed Hodge. "Why do you need steps?"

"Okay, if it's that simple, why isn't everyone creative. Perhaps I do over-analyse stuff, and maybe in your opinion I think a bit too logically sometimes, but I just want to see if I can define exactly what the creative process is. I'm due a holiday, so I'm taking the next two weeks off to do some research."

"Once you've discovered the creative process," said Hodge, "perhaps you can define how to be happy and what is the meaning of life."

Venn ignored him, used to his brother mocking his Spock-like brain.

"I know you think that my over-analysis of creativity will destroy it, but it's just something I want to find out about. I'll see you in two weeks."

"I can't wait," said Hodge, rubbing his hands in mock excitement. "Please, please, let there be a PowerPoint presentation."

5

It's the Waiting I can't Stand

"Every exit is an entry somewhere else."

Tom Stoppard

Hodge found the next two weeks much harder than he'd imagined. Being a twin, he'd always had a strong connection with his brother. But it wasn't just that he was missing his company; he was missing his input on ideas. The fact was, since they started working together, they'd always taken holidays at the same time. He was starting to realise that Venn did have a part to play in his creative process.

Normally, whenever he went to make himself a cup of tea, he'd ask Venn if he wanted a cup and then he'd stop and have a little chat about what he was working on. He always thought he was just passing the time of day, but now he realised that he was using Venn as a sounding board for his ideas. Without him there, Hodge found himself getting stuck and feeling blocked.

Relieved that the two weeks were over, Hodge was in the office at eight fifty. He normally rolled in at around ten, but Venn was always in at nine on the dot, and he wanted to be there to greet him. Nine o'clock came and went, and then ten, and still no sign of Venn. By half past ten, he was starting to get worried. He knew that it was pointless trying to phone him, as Venn had switched off his mobile and hadn't been staying at home. Hodge then remembered his brother had sent him an email after the first week to let him know that he was okay, so he switched on his computer to check his mail. There in his inbox were twenty identical emails from Venn saying, "So you're finding it hard without me, are you? I'm fine but I'm going to need another couple of weeks; there's a lot of stuff to digest."

Hodge felt frustrated that he was going to have to wait

another two weeks to see Venn, but there wasn't a lot he could do about it. He decided he wouldn't get much work done stuck in the office, so he'd take some time off himself as well. He thought he'd go to a few art galleries, see some movies and do some reading, use it as a time to recharge his batteries and get inspired.

6

A Man with a Plan

"Chance favours the prepared mind."

Louis Pasteur

Although Hodge really enjoyed the next two weeks, he still worried that he'd get another email from Venn saying he was going to take more time off. So he was very happy when he got back into the office and found Venn was already there.

"Missed me, have you?" said Venn.

"Not really," replied Hodge, trying to play it cool. "Just worried about all that business stuff you'll have piling up."

"Don't worry, I've been checking my emails. So are you interested to hear what I've discovered about the creative process?"

"Have you got a PowerPoint presentation for me?"

"No, I've got the next best thing … a list. There it is, above your desk."

Hodge looked above his desk and saw a framed list of five words:

1. INFORMATION

2. IMAGINATION

3. INCUBATION

4. ILLUMINATION

5. IMPLEMENTATION

He presumed that these were what Venn thought were the five stages of the creative process. He was interested to hear about them, but what he couldn't keep his eyes off was a picture next to it, with the words, "I'm not creative".

"I'm not creative? Is that meant to be about you or me?"

"Both of us," Venn said smiling.

"Look, I'm not trying to be arrogant, but surely you can't say that I'm not creative?"

"It'll make sense when I get to it, but you'll have to wait until the Incubation stage. Trust me, I think you'll find it interesting. It'll make you look at creativity in a completely different way."

"And you thought of this, did you?"

"Well I didn't think it, but then neither did anyone else. Out of all the people not thinking it, I was the closest one to not thinking it," said Venn.

"What are you on about?" said Hodge, actually starting to worry that the last month's 'researching' had slightly fried his brother's brain.

"Just hear me out. If after I've finished you still think it's rubbish, that's fine."

"Fire away, then."

"Okay, What makes mammals, and particularly humans, different from other animals?"

"I don't know? We don't hatch out of eggs?"

"Well that's true, but what I was actually thinking of was, we're the only ones with a neocortex."

"Whoa, there," cut in Hodge. "Neocortex! I don't want a lecture on neuroscience, I just want to know about the creative process."

"You can't talk about creativity without talking a bit about the brain. I promise that I won't make it too neurological. The neocortex, which is the wrinkly outer layer that makes the brain look like a walnut."

"Now you're talking my language."

"Anyway, what makes it so special is that it stops us just thinking one thought after another; instead it attaches all these different layers of associations to a concept or word. Of course, it's also the creator of metaphors, which are a great way for us to understand and explain complex ideas."

"How about giving me a metaphor, then, for what happens in the brain when you start thinking about something?"

Venn thought for a moment and then picked up an apple from a bowl of fruit on Hodge's desk.

"Okay, say you see an apple; you immediately starts making all these connections in your brain linked to apples."

"A bit like a tree with all its branches?"

"That's how I initially imagined it. But the branch structure of a tree is fixed, whereas in the brain, it's fluid, with neural pathways that are constantly changing. I think that a better way of looking at it is by imagining it's like a massive skyscraper with superfast lifts that connect all the floors of information. So, if someone tells you to think about an apple, the lifts whip up and down, accessing all of the information related to apples. This includes everything from types of apple to all of your memories and experiences linked with apples, as well as people or things connected with apples: Newton, William Tell, Adam and Eve, Apple Computers, Snow White and the poisoned apple, etc.

Say your mind latches onto William Tell and the story of him shooting the apple off his son's head. It's as if the lift had stopped at the 'William Tell' floor, and there would be everything you know related to William Tell. But of course, on that floor there are thousands of other lifts connecting to other information. From the William Tell floor, you take a lift related to everything you know about archery and bows and arrows. Before you know it, you've stopped on a floor with Cupid and his bow and arrow, and now you're connected to all of your thoughts on love. And that process, which takes milliseconds, is happening all the time in our brain. In one millisecond you've jumped from 'apple' to 'love'."

Venn waited for his brother to say something, but Hodge was deep in thought.

"It's funny," said Hodge after a few moments, "You saying 'apple' and 'love' made me think of New York. Then I thought why New York and I've just worked it out. 'The big apple' and the famous New York logo 'I♥NY'."

"There you go, thank you for being such a willing guinea pig. You've just shown it in action. You didn't consciously think, 'what do I associate with 'apple' and 'love', did you?"

"No, it just came into my head."

"Exactly. Although your conscious mind might have analysed how you got there, it was your unconscious that came up with the New York association. This is all happening in our unconscious, over which we have no control. It just offers us up ideas, and our conscious mind decides which ones to take notice of," said Venn. "Our conscious mind is the thinking part of the brain, and I've got a much simpler building in mind to use as a metaphor to represent that: our offices. Do you remember when we were kids and there was a cartoon strip called 'The Numskulls' where a man was controlled by lots of tiny people in different parts of his body?"

"Yeah, I remember. What was the name of that comic?"

"That doesn't matter; just imagine that we are two of those Numskulls."

"That won't be hard," said Hodge.

"Our offices are like the two sides of the brain. Mine is the left half, where the more logical analytical thought goes on, and yours is the right half, which is more about emotions and creativity. I think that when a lot of people think about creativity, they imagine it's all about getting in touch with your inner child, who would obviously live in your mess of an office. But research has actually shown that the most creative people are the ones with the strongest corpus callosum, the thick band of neural fibres at the base of the brain, which connects the two hemispheres. This shows that both sides of the brain play an important role in the creative process.

Some people seem to think we've all got an inner critic, which inhabits the left-hand side of our brain and is always judging. But if you think of it in relation to us, I hope you don't think that I hamper your creativity. I know that I'm always nagging you about deadlines, but I'd like to think I help you to finish things, as well as being a sounding board for your ideas. I hope I'm more of a manager than a critic."

"I have to admit, you being away for a month has made me realise that you definitely do play a part in my creative process," agreed Hodge.

7

Stage One: Information

"When the only tool you own is a hammer,
every problem begins to resemble a nail."

Abraham Maslow

Hodge looked up again at the framed line "I'm not creative" above his desk and then turned to Venn, who was still sitting on his sofa.

"Go on, then," he said, "I'm still waiting to find out why you think I'm not creative."

"I will get to that, I promise, but let me start with the first stage of the creative process, 'Information'. Now, I think a lot of people believe that being creative is all about having ideas. I certainly did. But filling your head full of the right information is just as vital. In fact, in a way, it's more important. If you haven't got enough information, you'll never come up with any good ideas. It doesn't matter whether you're a scientist or an artist, you need to be a sponge and soak up as much information as you can."

"What, any information?"

"Well, I'd split information into two types: specific and general. Specific information is about the problem that you are trying to solve, and general information is basically everything else. I've discovered that, like you, creative people are fascinated by the world around them. Leonardo Da Vinci called it 'curiosita' – 'an insatiably curious approach to life and unrelenting quest for continuous learning'."

"I can understand that you need specific information on what you're working on, but how does the general information fit in? Just describing it as 'everything else' seems a bit vague."

"The truth is, you can never know what general information will be useful. But if, like Leonardo Da Vinci, you're always curious and constantly soaking up information about the world around you, you'll have better foundations with which to build interesting ideas," said Venn. "Take Steve Jobs; he was really into computers as a kid, but after he dropped out of his course at college, he enrolled in a course on calligraphy. Although he didn't end up becoming a calligrapher, the beauty and balance of calligraphy had a huge influence on his attitude to product design at Apple.

You wouldn't think that studying butterflies would make you into a great novelist. But Vladimir Nabokov said that his interest in them helped him to develop his deep passion for detail and precision."

"That makes sense, I suppose, but how does this whole information gathering thing relate to me writing children's books?"

"Well, you've read hundreds of other people's children's books. That's all soaked up by your brain and gives background on structure, what works, what doesn't. You go to schools and read your stories and talk to the children about what they like and don't like. That's information. If you're interested in a subject, you'll just soak it up.

When Quentin Tarantino was asked if he went to film school, he said, 'No, I went to films'. In the same way, good writers read a great deal. Even if they couldn't write about story structure, they have unconsciously learnt about and understand it through all of the books they've read. Of course for any writer or artist, anything they've thought, felt or experienced in their life is, for them, 'general information' that then influences their work.

I think many people believe that information gathering is

boring and they want to rush on to the fun part of coming up with ideas. But the more time you spend on the problem, the more interesting and original your solution will be. Interrogate a problem like a three year old would. Every time one of your questions is answered, you ask 'why' again."

"But then," said Hodge, "whoever you're asking will just act like an irritated parent and say, 'Oh, just because …' to stop the continual questioning."

"Yes, but if you don't keep pushing and don't keep challenging what is accepted, you won't get breakthrough ideas:

'Why does a map have to be geographically correct?'

'Oh, just because.'

'Why does time always have to be constant?'

'Oh, just because.'

'Why do apples fall downwards?'

'Oh, just because.'

If those answers had been accepted, we would never have had the London Underground map as we know it, the theory of relativity and the theory of gravity."

"And think where we'd be without gravity."

8

Change Your Mind

"Every man can, if he so desires, become
the sculptor of his own brain."

Santiago Ramon y Cajal

Venn had never really been interested in all the 'stuff' that Hodge had strewn around his office. But since his voyage of discovery into the world of creativity, he was looking at it all in a new light. He picked up a book full of pictures of everyday objects – taps, bins, kitchen appliances, which, by the way they were photographed, looked like they had faces. Hodge smiled at his brother's new-found interest in his clutter.

"That's quite a funny book, isn't it?" said Hodge. "I found myself looking at objects very differently after reading that. It's one of those books that I flick through sometimes when I'm a bit stuck."

"I was going to talk about the next stage of the creative process, 'Imagination' now, but seeing that book reminded me of something else I was going to talk about regarding 'Information'. If you want to look at things differently, you need to freshen up what's in your head."

"I suppose that's what I was doing in the time you were away, going to art galleries and stuff like that."

"Exactly. I found out that the graphic designer, Stefan Sagmeister, closes his studio and takes a year off every seven years to fill his head and his staff's with new influences and stimuli to re-invigorate their minds," said Venn. "But from how he describes it, the time sounds more like a year on than a year off. He says that most of the ideas they come up with in the seven years after the sabbatical have originated in that year away from the office."

"So you're saying, it's like your head's a library and what

he's doing is changing all the books in it."

"So you might think," said Venn, smiling. "But a more realistic analogy would not just be replacing the books in the library, but actually changing the physical shape of the library itself."

"What?" said Hodge, screwing up his face in disbelief.

"I know it sounds strange, but it's true. Scientists call the phenomenon 'neural plasticity'. Everything you see, hear, touch, taste, smell and even your thoughts, all cause microscopic changes in the physical structure of your brain. Taking in new information and thinking new thoughts has the effect of literally 'changing your mind'."

"Really? I find that a bit hard to believe."

"I did, as well, but there are lots of examples to back it up. Take London taxi drivers. Compared to other people, they've been found to have a larger hippocampus."

"Is that the area of the brain that deals with being opinionated?" joked Hodge.

"No, it's the one that, amongst other things, deals with spatial awareness. Because they've spent so long learning the streets of London, the area of the brain that deals with navigation has actually grown.

Here's another example. There have been cases where people who'd lost the use of an arm through a stroke, were able to use it again in as little as ten days. The reason for this is that there's nothing actually wrong with the arm; it's the region of the brain that controls the arm that is damaged. By strapping up the stroke victim's good arm, a different region of the brain was forced to assume the function of the damaged part of the brain. You can also," added Venn, "make changes to your brain that normally require physical activity, without lifting a finger."

"Now you're talking my language," said Hodge.

"A study by Harvard Medical School took two groups and had them practise the piano for two hours a day. One group practised on a physical piano and the other group were only allowed to use mental practice. They would sit in front of a piano and imagine practising it, but they weren't allowed to touch the piano itself. Amazingly, exactly the same changes took place in the motor cortex of both groups. After three days, when the group doing the mental practice actually played a physical piano, their accuracy in playing was exactly the same as the group who had been practising on the real piano all along. Over an extended period, those practising on the physical piano did move ahead, but when given the chance to practice on a physical piano, the 'mental practice' group quickly caught up.

I also read about a violinist who spent seven years in jail without his violin, but practised mentally every single night. On the very night that he was released, he gave an impeccable performance on his violin. The imaginary motions that the violinist engaged in during his time in jail were able to build, or at least maintain, his fine motor skills."

"So, next time you see me sitting here doing nothing, I can tell you I'm practising the piano."

"You could if you knew how to play the piano in the first

place. Practising Chopsticks in your head isn't going to turn you into a concert pianist."

"Fair enough," conceded Hodge. "Okay, here's a thought. You know there's that Malcolm Gladwell theory about people needing 10,000 hours practice to become an expert at something. Do you think all that time spent concentrating on one thing re-shapes the brain?"

"I'm sure it does; that's probably why people get to a stage where they're almost doing it without thinking. Of course, that's great if you're playing sport or a musical instrument. But from a creative point of view, repetition can be a hindrance.

The whole point of creativity is to think differently. A certain thought creates a neural pathway and then, if you keep thinking that way, those neural pathways become neural motorways. The mind will always want to travel that way, because you'll get from A to B faster. But thinking faster is not always better, especially when it comes to creativity."

"Sometimes you want to take the scenic route."

"Scenic route; that's good," said Venn. "It's true, though; you'll come across much more interesting ideas than if you take the motorway. So it's not surprising that a lot of the great creative thinkers did their best thinking when they were young and their minds were free of neural motorways. Einstein had what was called his 'miracle year', or his miracle three and a half months, to be more precise, when he was just twenty-six. In that time, he wrote three papers, one which won him the Nobel prize, one which confirmed beyond doubt the existence and size of atoms and another which introduced the mind, space and time-bending concept of special relativity.

The trouble is; the left-hand side of the brain, which is all about logic, is there to make you learn from experience. It's there to stop you making the same mistake again and again. But that type of thinking can censor your creative thinking.

Say you wrote a children's book about spiders and it didn't sell very well. If you tried to write another book about spiders, I'd try to dissuade you from doing it. As a left-brained thinker, I'd just be using past experience to stop you wasting your time. I might be right, but there's also the possibility that the first book on spiders just wasn't a very good book and it had nothing to do with the spider element. Now, are you ready for a test to see if your thinking's stuck in a rut?"

"Does it involve spiders?" asked Hodge warily.

"No."

"Good. Go on, then."

"Okay, imagine there's a needle in a haystack. What creative ways could you use to find that needle?"

Hodge thought for a bit, determined to think of something clever to prove how un-rutty his thinking was. Then it came to him in a flash.

"Use a giant magnet!"

"Very good, very creative. How about burning down the haystack?"

"But ..."

"Caught you!" said Venn smiling. "Your thinking's in a rut.

No, let me re-phrase that, your thinking's in a 'but'. Did you say 'but' because you were thinking that the hay is something of value and shouldn't be destroyed?"

"I suppose so," agreed Hodge begrudgingly.

"Come on, you still came up with a really creative solution, I was just trying to show you how easily we can fall into a certain way of thinking through self-censorship. We're often not even aware that we're doing it."

"That's a bit depressing," said Hodge.

"It is, isn't it. But the good news is that if we make a concerted effort to do things differently, it will actually make us think more creatively. When I was reading various books on creativity in the last month, I found lots of them said that doing things differently would help boost your creativity. Things like having lunch with someone you wouldn't normally eat with, reading magazines outside your usual spectrum of interest, taking the bus instead of the train to work, that kind of thing. I always thought it was just creative fluff ..."

"Don't knock creative fluff, it's what pays both of our wages."

"... But it turns out," continued Venn, "that there's some real science behind it. If you can break your routine, you also break certain cognitive patterns. Well-travelled neural pathways are abandoned, forcing new connections to be made between brain cells. It's another way of getting you off the neural motorways and onto the scenic route.

The Dutch psychologist, Simone Ritter, calls this 'getting stuck in a rut' syndrome, 'functional fixedness'. In her test, she took a classic Dutch breakfast, bread and butter with chocolate sprinkles on it, and quite literally turned it on its head. The students followed prompts from a computer while making their breakfast. Instead of shaking chocolate sprinkles onto the buttered bread, they were instructed to put the sprinkles on the plate and then place the buttered bread, butter side down, onto the sprinkles. They still ended up with bread and butter with chocolate sprinkles on it. It's just that the method they used to get there was very unorthodox. After doing this test, the students took classic creativity tests and were found to have increased their creativity by up to 15%."

"And their waistlines by 10%," added Hodge.

"Probably. But it really made me think about how malleable the brain is. It's as if it's a lump of sculptor's clay that is constantly being shaped and re-shaped by all of our thoughts and actions, whether conscious or unconscious. Don't you think that's incredible?"

"Sorry?"

"I've lost you, haven't I? You've drifted off into a world of bread and butter with chocolate sprinkles, haven't you?"

"I'm afraid so."

Venn sighed. He really wanted Hodge to listen carefully to what he had to say, so he decided that it would be good to have a break.

"I can't offer you chocolate sprinkles, but how about a cup of tea and some chocolate biscuits?"

"Sounds good to me."

As they walked to the kitchen, Hodge turned to his brother.

"I was listening, you know. And I do think it's amazing your brain can change. Mind you, it makes me think that all those pointless daydreams I have are probably turning my brain to jelly."

"Don't be so sure. I actually think that daydreams play a very important role in creativity, but I'll get on to that later."

9

Stage Two: Imagination

"Think left and think right and think low and think high.
Oh, the thinks you can think up if only you try."

Dr. Seuss

Once they'd had their tea and devoured half a packet of chocolate biscuits, Venn continued.

"Okay, so once you feel that you've taken in as much information as you can on a subject, it's time to move on to Stage Two, 'Imagination'.

This is the stage where you give the right-hand side of your brain free rein. You want to think of as many ideas as you can and be as non-judgemental as possible. Going back to the analogy of our offices being like the left and right-hand sides of the brain, this is the stage where you'd lock the door and let your right-brained mind run free. The last thing you want, is me popping my head round the door with my logical brain shooting down ideas for being impractical. Believe it or not, there is actually a scientific reason why this idea-generating stage is more of a right-brained activity."

"I thought there might be. Go, right brain!"

"It's because the right-hand side of the brain is actually wired differently.

The dendrites, the parts of the neurons that collect information, generally branch out much further in the right hemisphere, so each neuron in the right-hand side of the brain is collecting information from a broader source. This allows them to make much more surprising and interesting connections."

"Is it a bit like asking a question to the whole country rather than just the people in your town?"

"Yeah, that's a good way of looking at it. But the really important part of this 'Imagination' stage is not to worry too much about whether your ideas are good or not: the aim is to have as many ideas as you can, to really believe that you've emptied your head of ideas. You want to feel like you've hit a wall and can't think of anything else.

One of the classic traps, especially for people new to creative thinking like me, is to fall in love with one of your first ideas and feel that you've cracked it, at which point you stop thinking about the problem. The double Nobel prize winning chemist, Linus Pauling, said, 'the best way to have a good idea is to have a lot of ideas'."

"I know what you mean about getting hooked on one of your first thoughts. I often get fixated on ideas I have early on, but then after I've spent more time thinking, I realise that those first ideas weren't that great after all. It's funny, but it's usually the ideas you come up with at the end which are the best ones."

"The other thing I found was that an idea that seems silly at the time can often spark something else off later on. So it's good to make a note of everything you think of. Many creative people carry notebooks around with them. I'm sure there's nothing worse than that feeling of having a great idea and then not being able to remember what it is later on."

"I'd definitely agree with that," said Hodge. "But what about those times when you can't think of anything?"

"Well, when I tried to write that children's story and couldn't come up with any ideas, I felt like I was pretty useless and totally uncreative. But now, having read a lot about creativity, I realise that it's just part of the process."

"Are you saying it's good to have writer's block?" asked Hodge, with a look of disbelief.

"You say it like it's some kind of disease."

"Believe me; when you're a writer, it is."

"I think it's something writers have conjured up as an excuse for not doing the hard job of just sitting down at their desk and writing, or at least trying to write. Think of all the people who say that they've got an idea for a book, but have never written it."

"Tell me about it. Every book signing I do, I get people saying they've got this great idea for a book. I tell them they should sit down and write it, but I'm sure that 95% of them never do."

"Exactly, and that's because it's not easy. Loads of people have ideas in their heads that they think would make a great story. But even if you've got an idea that seems to work perfectly in your head, it can be a different matter trying to get it down on paper. I read about a lot of well-known writers saying that they'll look for any distraction to put off having to write: sharpening pencils, answering emails, tidying their office. In your mind, you want to write, but there's also part of you that knows it's going to be hard work and encourages you to procrastinate."

"True," nodded Hodge.

"I think that the people who actually become writers are the ones who are prepared to chain themselves to the desk. I liked what the writer, Maya Angelou, said about it: 'What I do is write. I may write for two weeks "the cat sat on the mat, that is that, not a rat." And it might be just the most boring and awful stuff. But I try. When I'm writing, I write. And then it's as if the muse is convinced that I'm serious and says, "Okay, okay, I'll come"". Of course," added Venn, "just because you force yourself to sit down and write, doesn't mean you're going to write a masterpiece. But even if you've just got an average idea, you've got more chance of success than the genius who never puts pen to paper. I realise now that no one is naturally creative. You've got to put the hours in."

"I know it's important, as you say, to 'put the hours in', but in my experience, forcing yourself to stay sitting at the desk isn't always the answer. In fact, I saw a good quote in the paper about it that I cut out. Where is it?"

Hodge started rummaging in a box of newspaper clippings, eventually pulling out what he was looking for.

"Here you go," said Hodge. "I'll see your Maya Angelou and raise you a Hilary Mantel. This is what she had to say about it: 'If you get stuck, get away from your desk. Take a walk, take a bath, go to sleep, make a pie, draw, listen to music, meditate, exercise; whatever you do, don't just stick there scowling at the problem. But don't make telephone calls or go to a party; if you do, other people's words will pour in where your lost words should be. Open a gap for them, create a space. Be patient'."

Venn said nothing for a few seconds and then held out his hand so that he could have a look at the quote himself. Venn quietly read the quote and then looked back at Hodge.

"That's a great quote; it perfectly illustrates the next stage of the creative process. 'Be patient' she says, that's because you're waiting for an idea. This is very important, because you're not in control of when the idea will come. I think people often confuse being blocked with the Incubation stage."

"You mean that disheartening feeling that you can't think of anything?"

"That's the one! Although it feels like you're not thinking, this is when your unconscious mind kicks into gear and really starts working on the problem in earnest. Your conscious mind spends a lot of time thinking about inconsequential things like what you're going to have for lunch, what you're going to do when you get home from work, that kind of stuff. Stuff that your unconscious knows is not really worth working on."

"I wouldn't say that what I have for lunch is at all inconsequential, but I take your point,' said Hodge "Your unconscious wants to feel your conscious mind has been sweating it out on a problem before it deems it as something worthy of working on."

"Yeah, I think that's a good way of putting it. It's like that Maya Angelou quote, where she says she might have to write 'rubbish' for a couple of weeks before her muse sees that she's serious and starts to help out."

"So, you're saying that your 'muse' is your unconscious?"

"Certainly in the way we use the word now. The ancient Greeks thought of them as real, but I'll talk about that later. But, yeah, your muse, your intuition, hunches, inspiration, it's all comes from your unconscious."

10
Stage Three: Incubation

"Creativity comes from conscious facts planted in the unconscious and allowed to germinate."

Bertrand Russell

Venn noticed that Hodge was looking up at the picture with the words "I'm not creative" on it.

"I know that you're dying to find out why I don't think you're creative, but just let me explain the Incubation stage first," said Venn.

"Okay, go on, then."

"So, in the Imagination stage, you've thought of as many ideas as you can and now you feel like you've hit a brick wall. Your conscious mind is stumped, so your unconscious takes over."

"But I wouldn't know that, would I, because it's in my unconscious, right?"

"Exactly. You're feeling drained and full of self-doubt. But the important thing is to still keep the desire to crack whatever the problem is you're thinking about. If your conscious mind loses interest in the problem, so will your unconscious."

"So, what do you do?"

"Good question. You don't want to stress too much about not being able to solve the problem, but at the same time you don't want to totally forget about it. You want to keep the mind gently stimulated."

Venn picked up the Hilary Mantel quote that Hodge had shown him earlier.

"Listen to the end of this Hilary Mantel quote again, 'Whatever you do, don't just stick there scowling at the problem. But don't make telephone calls or go to a party; if you do, other people's words will pour in where your lost words should be. Open a gap for them, create a space. Be patient.' It's like what I was saying; it's important that your conscious mind isn't over-stimulated by challenging tasks or engaging conversations that are totally unrelated to your creative problem. If it is, your unconscious, will think you're not really that interested in finding a solution to the problem.

At the other end of the spectrum, you don't want to be totally zoned out watching brainless TV or videos of cats skateboarding on the Internet. You want to be doing what I'd call 'Goldilocks thinking': neither too hard, nor too soft. Something that you can almost do without thinking, like mowing the lawn, going for a walk, having a shower. It's as if you're on automatic pilot. Agatha Christie said, 'the best time for planning a book is while you're doing the dishes'."

"I do hope you've got some scientific evidence to back this up," joked Hodge, knowing that his brother would have just that.

Venn smiled, "Yes. Professor Jonathan Schooler of the University of California, Santa Barbara, has done an experiment on this. He took three groups of people and gave them a minute to think of as many unusual uses for a house brick as they could. They were all then given a minute's rest. While they rested, the first group was told to just sit there and think of nothing. The second had the simple and unchallenging task of sorting Lego bricks by colour and the third had to build a house with the Lego. After that, they were all given another minute to think of some more uses for a house brick.

The group that did the best was the second one, whose

minds were mildly stimulated. The first group, who were given nothing to do, lost themselves in conscious thought, thinking about things like what they were going to have for dinner, that kind of thing. The third group, who were given the task of building a house, had to focus their attention on what sort of house to build and what pieces they would need. The middle group had a mindless task that gently occupied their conscious mind. This left most of their brains' processing power to be diverted to the unconscious to come up with more creative uses for a brick."

"So when I've thought of as many ideas as I can, do I just go and stand in a shower and wait for the light-bulb moment to happen?"

"No, I think you're more likely to turn into a prune before any moment of insight hits you," said Venn. "If you're thinking about getting that moment of insight, then you probably won't. You might even need to take in some more information and try to think of some more ideas, and then, when you least expect it, the breakthrough will suddenly happen."

"For someone who's a left-brained thinker, I thought you'd have come up with a process which you had a bit more control over."

"I'd love it if it was a bit more regimented, but it is what it is. Actually, that lack of control you have over when you come up with your big idea is what I was getting at when I gave you that 'I'm not creative' picture. In fact, it's not just you; it's why no one is creative."

"Oh, just lump me in with the other seven billion people

on this planet, why don't you?"

"Well, we are all similar in a lot of ways," said Venn. "The concept of 'the self' is very ingrained in us, so naturally when an idea comes into your head, you believe that you've thought it. Of course, the ideas have come from your brain, but those great creative breakthroughs, those moments of genius weren't 'thought' by you; they bubble up from the unconscious where there is no thought and therefore no self. 'You' don't think of an idea, you just create the conditions for creativity to happen. Once an idea is in our conscious minds, then it can be shaped and analysed but the germ of the idea comes from our unconscious.

Everyone says that it's the conscious mind that makes us special. But it's the huge processing power of the unconscious and the random associations it makes that are the vital part of being creative. You could say the conscious mind makes us human; the unconscious mind makes us creative."

11

Your Other Mind

"The intuitive mind is a sacred gift and the rational mind is a faithful servant. We have created a society that honours the servant and has forgotten the gift."

Albert Einstein

Hodge sat there, looking into space, and then turned to Venn.

"I do kind of get what you're saying; I just find it a bit depressing that all the great ideas throughout history haven't been 'thought up', but have been processed by some huge computer-like machine."

Venn laughed to himself as he listened to his brother moan.

"What's so funny?" said Hodge.

"You're just taking such an emotional, right-brained view of the whole thing. It's as if you're jealous of your own unconscious."

"Yeah, trust you, Mr. analytical left-brain, to side with the robot."

"You seem to think the unconscious is just like some huge super computer, but it's not at all. The brain transmits information at the relatively feeble rate of about 200 mph, compared to computer chips that transmit at the speed of light. Our brains also get tired and don't always function exactly as we want them to. You wouldn't get a computer forgetting important bits of information, would you?"

"I don't know. My computer seems to do a good job of it."

"But what makes the brain special compared to the computer is that each one of its hundred billion neurons can connect to any other. Computers have relatively few active pathways at work at any given time, whereas we have millions, which can give rise to infinite permutations. Also, while a computer makes clear connections, we often get crossed wires, which in a computer would be seen as a fault, but in the brain is an aid to creative thought, creating more unusual and surprising results. The only trouble is that when it feels like our brain's not working, we can't switch it off and on again, can we?"

"That's true," agreed Hodge.

"That's why we need sleep. Just think how often people get stuck on a problem or issue and say 'let's sleep on it'. Alexander Graham Bell said 'Often, what was dark and perplexing you the night before, is found to be perfectly solved the next morning'."

"Yeah, I would agree with that."

"Sometimes we don't even have to wait until the morning to have our problems solved," continued Venn. "We can get the answers in our dreams, which also give us a glimpse into the unconscious at work. Paul McCartney said that the melody for 'Yesterday' came to him in a dream and Robert Louis Stevenson came up with the idea for Dr Jekyll And Mr Hyde while he was asleep. And following an evening reading ghost stories and a challenge set by Lord Byron to come up with her own ghost story, Mary Shelley dreamt of the idea for Frankenstein."

"I think that the technical term for that is constructive nightmare."

"Sometimes, the breakthrough idea can be hidden in a dream. Elias Howe who invented the sewing machine, said that he'd already had the idea of a machine with a needle which would go through a piece of cloth, but he couldn't figure out exactly how it would work. In his dream, cannibals were preparing to cook him and they were dancing around the fire waving their spears. Howe noticed at the head of each spear there was a small hole through the shaft. The up and down motion of the spear and the hole near the head, stayed with him when he woke. The idea of passing the thread through the needle close to the point, not at the other end was the major innovation that made mechanical sewing possible. I think that's why a lot of creative people keep a paper and pen by their bedside to write down any ideas that they come up with in the night."

"I find that time first thing in the morning when you're half asleep is quite good for ideas," added Hodge.

"Maybe because you are half asleep, you're not really thinking much, so it's easier to hear the ideas bubbling up from your unconscious."

"Yeah, let's not take any glory away from Mr clever clogs, the unconscious."

Venn ignored his brother and carried on.

"You know, even a short sleep in the day has been proved to help you to be more creative."

"At last," said Hodge, "Now I can put afternoon naps down as work on my time sheet."

"You don't do time sheets."

"Okay then, when it's 3 o'clock in the afternoon and I've got my feet on the desk and my eyes closed, perhaps you won't stand at the door to my office, pretending to clear your throat."

"Yeah, I might think twice about it now. At the University of California, San Diego, they did a test with two groups of volunteers who were asked to mull over a creative problem. One group quietly rested whereas the other group actually slept. They found that the ones who entered REM during sleep improved their creative problem-solving ability by almost forty per cent."

"Forty per cent! I'm certainly going to do a lot more sleeping from now on."

"It's pretty impressive, isn't it? Now, before we talk about the next stage of the creative process, I want to talk about your battle with the unconscious."

"Oh, come on, I was only joking."

"I think you were half joking. I still think your ego; your conscious mind, finds it hard to accept that it hasn't 'thought' of an idea. It's natural to want to feel in control of our thoughts; it's what gives us a sense of identity. But we're a lot less in control than we think. I'll show you, if you're prepared to take part in a little brain experiment."

"You're not going to cover my head in electrodes are you?"

"No, don't worry. All I want you to do is close your eyes and think of a red car for a minute. Try not to think of anything else, just a red car."

"For one minute," said Hodge, visibly relieved. "No problem."

A minute later, Hodge opened his eyes.

"How did you get on?" asked Venn.

"That was one long minute. Every time I tried to picture a red car, it would be okay for a few seconds and then some strange thought would barge its way into my head."

"See, you're not as in control of your thoughts as you imagined, are you? Okay, now try something a bit easier. I want you to spend another minute with your eyes closed, but this time I want you to think of anything, anything at all, except for a red car."

"Easy, peasy."

"Off you go, then."

Another minute passed and then Venn told his brother he could open his eyes.

"So, how did you get on?"

"Actually, that was a bit scary. I started to think about my latest children's book and then this red car would keep forcing its way into my thoughts. However hard I tried to get it out, it kept popping back in. That was very strange."

"You see, that's your unconscious offering things up to you, and it's the job of your conscious mind to decide which one to take hold of. Even though the idea is not to think of a red car, you have given the image of a red car an importance, so your unconscious keeps offering you images of red cars. Here's another example. Now just think of the answers quickly and don't ponder too much."

"Okay."

"What's a common abbreviation for Coca-Cola? What do we call the sound a frog makes? What is a comedian's funny story called? What do you call the white of an egg? Now, what was your answer for the egg?"

"Yolk," said Hodge.

"That's what I answered when I first heard it, but of course the 'yolk' is the yellow of the egg. If I asked you that on its own, you'd never get it wrong. But when you answer things without really thinking about it, it's your unconscious feeding you the answer. It's looking for patterns and connections in things, so because the previous answers 'Coke, croak, joke' have all rhymed and it knows that part of the egg is called the 'yolk', it assumes that this is the right answer. It's known as priming."

"Not so clever now, are you, unconscious?" said Hodge.

Venn shook his head and then continued.

"Of course, if your conscious mind spent time thinking about it logically, it would come up with the correct answer. But when you answer it quickly, without thinking, your unconscious has to come up with a solution from the information it's been given. Ideas won't always be delivered to you fully formed by your unconscious. Our conscious mind has to knock them into shape. Imagine your brain is like the sea."

"I'm trying to, but the tide's out."

"Your brain is like the sea, with everything unconscious being under the surface. On the seabed are hundreds and thousands of oysters. To get a beautiful pearl to grow in them is a bit like getting an idea to grow in your unconscious. To get a pearl to grow, you need a bit of grit to agitate the oyster. To get an idea to grow, you need a conscious desire for a solution to a problem to agitate the unconscious into action. When the idea becomes fully formed, it's like a beautiful pearl.

Now, imagine that, as the oyster opens, the pearl turns into a bubble and rises to the surface. When it reaches the surface, your conscious mind has a chance of seeing it, but the bubble only stays on the surface for a split second before it bursts and is gone. Your conscious mind has to be ready to catch it."

"Pearls of wisdom."

"That's good. Did you just think of that?" said Venn, always impressed with his brother's creative associations.

"It just popped into my head."

"So you didn't think it, then?"

"What are you on about?" replied a confused Hodge.

"Think about what you just said, 'It just popped into my head'. You didn't think it. Your unconscious was fed the information about a pearl and ideas forming and came up with the connection 'pearls of wisdom'. We take phrases like 'it just popped into my head' for granted, but it's actually a very good description of how it feels when the unconscious delivers an idea to the conscious mind."

12

Stage Four: Illumination

"This is the extraordinary thing about creativity:
If you keep your mind resting against the subject in a
friendly way, sooner or later you will get a reward
from your unconscious."

John Cleese

"Fancy a walk?" said Venn.

"Yeah, I could do with some fresh air, my head hurts."

The two brothers didn't have far to go, as they had a large park opposite their office. As they walked round the perimeter footpath, Hodge turned to his brother.

"Go on then, tell me on the next stage of the process."

"Okay. The fourth stage is Illumination. Also known as 'the eureka moment', 'the aha moment', 'the light-bulb moment', 'the moment of insight'. It's no surprise that it's always described as a moment in time, because just as electricity lights up a bulb, a flash of energy actually surges through the brain at the point of insight. That's why it has such a powerful effect; you actually 'feel' the idea."

Venn took a newspaper cutting out of his pocket.

"This is how J.K. Rowling described getting the idea for her first book for adults: 'I had a totally physical response you get to an idea that you know will work. It's a rush of adrenaline; it's chemical. I had it with Harry Potter and I had it with this.' Interestingly, she says she had the idea for 'The Casual Vacancy' on a plane and the idea for 'Harry Potter' on a train.

Scientists have found that the moment of insight is accompanied by a spike in brainwaves called gamma waves, the highest electrical frequency generated by the brain. They erupt in one spot in the right hemisphere of the brain, just above the ear, called the Anterior Superior Temporal Gyrus."

"Catchy name," said Hodge.

Ignoring his brother, Venn continued. "Cognitive

neuroscientist, Professor John Kounios, has also used brain scans to look at what happens in the brain before the gamma spike. He says, 'A second before the "aha" moment, there's a burst of alpha waves in the back of the head on the right side. Now, strangely enough, the back of the brain accomplishes visual processing and alpha is known to reflect brain areas shutting down'."

"I suppose it's like when people are lost in thought, they're described as having 'their eyes glazed over', because their mind doesn't want to take in visual information," said Hodge. "Maybe it's also why when musicians and singers perform, they often have their eyes closed. They're trying to concentrate their mind on really 'feeling' the music."

"Yes, I think it might be. At least half of the brain is devoted directly or indirectly to vision. It's been found that when trying to remember something or solve a problem, people will avoid looking at faces and will look down or stare into space.

But as well as the part of the brain involved in visual processing closing down, neuropsychologist, Rex Jung, studied brain scans of people as they let their minds wander. He noticed a distinct change in the frontal lobes, which are the main areas of consciousness in the brain. They were almost going into sleep mode, which he calls 'transient hypofrontality'."

"Just trying to spell that would send my brain into sleep mode," said Hodge.

"Doctor Charles Limb, who's done brain scans on jazz musicians while they improvise, said, 'To promote that ability to take risks, they have to turn off a little bit of the gatekeeper. So we saw this shut down of the pre-frontal cortex in these musicians.' He also found similar results in other improvising creatives, like illustrators, cartoonists and freestyle rappers. Einstein said that his breaks in work to play the violin and especially the periods of improvisation, lead to some of his greatest scientific insights."

"So let me get this right; you're saying that your visual processing and the chatter of your conscious mind are being shut down so that you can fully concentrate on being creative?"

"Precisely. The important thing for creativity is not what you need to switch on in your mind, but what you need to switch off. It's all about quieting your thoughts, which I think is why meditation is often cited as something that helps creativity. Professor John Kounios said, 'People who tend to solve problems with insight have a lower base level of frontal lobe activity. In other words, their frontal lobes are not controlling them or focusing them as much'."

"So, you're saying the frontal lobes of our brain, which are full of all our conscious chatter, act as sort of mental handcuffs."

"Mindcuffs."

"Yeah, mindcuffs. I like that," said Hodge laughing.

"It's like daydreaming; you're not really taking in what you're looking at. You're in a kind of trance."

"A creative trance! Imagine if daydreaming was re-named a 'creative trance'. People wouldn't think staring out of the window was a waste of time any more, would they? See, that's all that daydreaming needs, some good PR."

"You're right," agreed Venn. "But I don't think it's just daydreaming that brings on this 'creative trance' I think any activity which you can almost do on autopilot, can have the same effect. Activities like driving, taking a shower, mowing the lawn, washing the dishes, walking …"

"Walking! I knew it. You lured me out here with the promise of a gentle stroll round the park, when really you wanted to put me into some kind of hypnotic trance where I'd accept all your ideas without question."

"You've seen through my not so cunning plan," said Venn smiling.

"You're right though, they're all activities where you don't really have to think much about what you're doing and can easily become lost in your thought."

"That's an interesting phrase isn't it, 'lost in thought', I think it would be more accurate to call it 'lost in thoughts', because I don't think you're really thinking. You're wandering aimlessly through a forest of your own ideas and musings."

"And you said you're not creative? 'A forest of your own ideas and musings', I like that," said Hodge. "Actually, talking about musings, you know what I was thinking about earlier; what did people show to illustrate someone having an idea before the light-bulb was invented? A candle above someone's head?"

"I don't know, but it's a good question," replied Venn. "But what I do know, is that the ancient Greeks wouldn't have depicted anything above someone's head. They never even saw the original eureka moment, as a 'eureka' moment!"

"What are you on about?"

"You know that Archimedes coined the phrase when he jumped out of the bath after a moment of realisation that water displacement could be used to measure the volume of an object?"

"Yes."

"Well, in ancient Greece, they really didn't believe that individuals were creative; they saw it as inspiration from the gods. When Plato was asked, 'Will we say, of a painter, that he makes something?' he answered, 'Certainly not, he merely imitates'. Creative people these days joke about 'waiting for their muse' when they can't think of an idea. But the Greeks believed that the Muses were real. To them, they were goddesses who were considered the source of all knowledge, which was then invoked by the writer or artist.

Take the word 'genius'. It actually comes from ancient Rome and doesn't refer to a gifted individual, but a guiding spirit. The achievements of exceptional people were seen as an indication of the presence of a particularly powerful 'genius'. In fact, it was only during the Renaissance in the 14th century that creativity was first seen as the ability of a gifted individual."

"Do you think that's because in ancient Greece and Rome, no one really understood how the brain worked," said Hodge, "so when an idea popped into their head, they believed that it had been planted there by a higher force?"

"Definitely. I actually think that throughout the ages creative people have often been mystified as to where they get their ideas from. I read that William Blake, when describing his experience of writing the long narrative poem 'Milton', said: 'I have written this poem from immediate dictation, twelve or sometimes twenty lines at a time without premeditation and even against my will'."

"I wish that my unconscious would dictate some ideas to me. I'd be happy to be its glorified secretary if it could come up with great fully formed stories."

"I think that's the thing, isn't it; the majority of ideas don't come fully formed, do they," said Venn.

"You're right, I often think of my ideas as like decaying jigsaws. If I don't write them down straight away, pieces will fade and then eventually disappear altogether."

"Sometimes these 'light-bulb moments' are only the germ of a great idea and that's where the next stage, 'Implementation' comes in: making the idea as strong as it can possibly be and then making it happen."

13

Stage Five: Implementation

"The guy who invented the first wheel was an idiot.
The guy who invented the other three was a genius."

Sid Caesar

Back in their office, they sat down in their usual seats; Venn on the sofa, Hodge at his desk.

"I feel better for that fresh air," said Hodge. "Continue."

"Okay, so you've got a great idea, but it's not fully formed. This is when your conscious mind has an important role to play again. It's the final stage of the creative process, 'Implementation'.

When an idea floats up from your unconscious, it can be very fragile. It needs to be nurtured and strengthened. As soon as it gets out into the big wide world, there are bound to be critics, so until it's fully formed you need a supportive team around you. I think that this is when the left-hand side of the brain plays an important role. The right-hand side of the brain has already had the fun of creating the idea in conjunction with the unconscious, so if an idea isn't totally working, the right-hand side can lose interest and want to move on to thinking about something else."

"That's true. I know when I've had an idea for a children's story but can't get it to work, you've pushed me and I usually get there in the end," said Hodge.

"It's all very well coming up with a brilliant idea in your head, but it only becomes a truly great idea when you make it happen. This is the stage when it's good to get feedback and input from other people who you respect and trust. Ideas that come up with a revolutionary solution to a problem will often receive a lot of opposition initially, like Harry Beck's London Underground map."

"I've heard that in Hollywood, they say that everyone wants to be the first person to do something second."

"That doesn't surprise me," said Venn. "Especially when there's money involved, people get scared of taking risks. You've also got to be really determined and believe in your idea.

Everyone is aware of Edison as a great inventor, but fewer people are aware of his brilliant competitor, Nikola Tesla. In the 1890s, his AC power distribution beat Edison's DC power, to provide electricity for the whole of America.

He was the more gifted of the two and could picture whole inventions in his head. He could then make them without ever needing to create a blueprint. But he wasn't as driven as Edison. After Edison died, this is how Tesla described him: 'He had no hobby, cared for no sort of amusement of any kind and lived in utter disregard of the most elementary rules of hygiene'."

"Not good news when you think that Edison believed genius involved 1% inspiration and 99% perspiration," added Hodge.

"True," said Venn laughing. "Tesla also went on to say about Edison, 'His method was inefficient in the extreme, for an immense ground had to be covered to get anything at all unless blind chance intervened and, at first, I was almost a sorry witness of his doings, knowing that just a little theory and calculation would have saved him 90% of the labour'."

"But it's Edison who we remember, is that what you're saying?"

"Yes. As Edison said: 'Many of life's failures are people who did not realise how close they were to success when they gave up'."

"But what if it's not an invention, what if it's some artistic project. How do you know when to stop painting?"

"That's a good point. Whatever it is, you can keep polishing and polishing your idea. I think sometimes people can use this as a safety net."

"You mean, the kind of attitude that if you never finish something, you can never be criticised?"

"Exactly. But it's better to create something that isn't a great success, than never create anything at all. You need to get your idea out there. As Steve Jobs said, 'Real artists ship'."

14

Creative Craft

"The object isn't to make art, it is to be in that wonderful state which makes art inevitable."

Robert Henri

Hodge leant back in his chair and turned to Venn.

"You have been busy; I'm impressed. I've just got one question. I can see how these five stages describe creative thinking, but what about creative people like artists, musicians and dancers? They don't necessarily have to come up with 'the big idea' to be creative. Do you really think the unconscious has such an influence on their work?"

"That's something I've also thought quite a bit about: how you define what's creative and what isn't. I think, whether it's science, where you have only one answer, or the arts and business where there are infinite possibilities, it's all about going on a journey of discovery. You're going into uncharted territory, trying to create something new."

"Are you saying that every creative idea should have a big red starburst with the word 'NEW' on it?"

"In a way, yes. Even if you are developing an idea started by someone else, or merging different ideas, you are creating something new. Being original is central to creativity."

"Fair enough, but going back to my question about performers, they're not always following a creative thinking process are they?"

"Well, I think you'd be surprised," said Venn fishing a notebook out of his pocket. "Take this quote from Fred Astaire about creating a new dance routine with his choreographer: 'For maybe a couple of days we wouldn't get anywhere, just stand in front of the mirror and fool around. Then suddenly I'd get an idea or one of us would get an idea, so then we'd get started. You might get practically the whole idea of the routine done that day, but then you'd work on it, edit it, scramble it, and so forth. It might take sometimes as long as two, three weeks to get something going'."

"Okay, I can understand that creative thinking's involved in coming up with an idea for a dance or, say, writing a song, but what about musicians just improvising, or an artist just sitting down and painting a picture?"

Venn thought for a moment.

"Obviously there's a lot more 'creative craft' than 'creative thinking', but I still think the unconscious is involved, and that's what makes it creative. An improvising jazz musician has spent years learning to play, and when he improvises, as I discussed earlier, his brain is muting the chatter of his conscious mind. He's creating something original that's coming straight from his unconscious.

Take the famous line from Picasso where he said he that spent his whole life learning to draw like a child. Do you think that means a picture by a five year old is as creative as a picture by Picasso?"

"No, I don't think so."

"Even if the pictures looked almost identical?"

"No, because all of Picasso's experience would be in his."

"Exactly. It's like my description of an oily puddle glinting in the sunlight when I was a child. I wasn't saying it was 'like' a dead rainbow, I really thought it was a dead rainbow. Obviously, that makes it all the cuter, but it doesn't make it creative. Creativity is about looking at something in a different way and making new connections. It's like a child's dot-to-dot picture. It can be whatever you want it to be. You've just got to learn to ignore the numbers."

"I can't argue with that," said Hodge.

"Well, then," smiled Venn, "I think my work here is done. I'm off to my office, I've got lots of accounts to catch up on."

Hodge couldn't believe what his brother had just said.

"You've discovered all this about creativity and you're going off to work on spreadsheets?"

"I'm not turning my back on creativity, but I've realised that I enjoy my job, and there are always problems to solve in it. Look at double-entry book keeping; that was a great creative solution to a problem."

"Seriously, though, learning all about these great creative minds hasn't made you think differently about what you want to do? It hasn't changed your mind?"

"Oh yes, it's changed my mind," said Venn, smiling. "My mind is changed."

Summary

I really hope this book has given you a good understanding of what it means to be creative. Here's a reminder of the five stages of the creative process again:

1. Information. The information you take in creates the raw material for your ideas. The more you take in, the more interesting and innovative your ideas are likely to be. At this stage, it's also natural that your mind will want to run onto the fun part of coming up with ideas, but it's important to really analyse the question/problem. Better questions will create better answers, so keep asking 'why, why, why'.

One thing to remember: being creative is a very fluid thing. Ideas can pop up at any time. You can be in the first stage of collecting information, and an idea can suddenly come to you. This is a good sign: your unconscious sees that you're serious about solving this problem, and it's not going to wait on the sidelines until the Incubation Stage. It's going to start throwing ideas into the mix straight away. The only danger is that it's easy to get distracted and move on to thinking about ideas when you should still be trying to collect more information. Make a note of the idea you've just had, and then go back to collecting information.

It's important to remember that 'information' in a creative context, isn't just hard facts, but also relates to anything that's taken in by your five senses. So when you're researching a subject, don't just keep your nose in a book or glued to a computer screen. What you hear, what you see, what you experience, can all provide invaluable information. Architects have created buildings that stay cool without air conditioning, inspired by the self-cooling mounds created by termites. James Dyson got the idea for how his revolutionary vacuum cleaner would work by seeing how a sawmill extracted sawdust. When Einstein worked at the patent office in Bern, the nearby train station and the constant arrival and departure of trains inspired one of his famous thought experiments about time.

When you finally feel that there's no more information to be discovered in regard to the problem you're working on, it's time to move on to the Imagination Stage and start thinking of solutions.

2. Imagination. The Imagination Stage is where it's really important to be as non-judgemental as you can and try to think of as many ideas as possible. Always keep a record of all your ideas, as something that can initially seem silly can be the spark for a great idea later on. Also, try not to get too attached to any idea you have early on and think you've cracked it. If your conscious mind thinks that the problem's solved, your unconscious will just take the day off. And believe me, if you want to come up with great ideas, you'll want the processing power of your unconscious mind on board.

It may seem obvious, but it's also really important to have a strong desire to find a solution to whatever you're working on. Whether it's artistic, scientific or business orientated, you've got to be a little bit obsessed. If you're not, again, your unconscious won't bother getting involved.

There will then come a point where you feel that you can't think of anything else. You've come up with some okay ideas, but nothing really great, and now you feel as if you've hit a bit of a brick wall. This can be very de-motivating; you feel blocked and lost any ability to think creatively. It's natural to feel like giving up if you don't realise that this is just part of the creative process. Now it's time for the next stage, Incubation.

3. Incubation. This is the start of the unconscious phase of the creative process, which takes in Stages Three and Four, 'Incubation' and 'Illumination'. It's easy to get stressed and beat yourself up at this stage because you feel as if you can't think of anything, but that's the last thing you want to do. Getting stressed won't get you anywhere. Keep the problem percolating in your mind, but don't think about it excessively. John Cleese described this as, 'keeping your mind resting against the subject in a friendly way'.

Keep it on the back burner. You're aware of it, but your

conscious mind isn't focusing on the problem. Sometimes you will have to go back to the first two stages and take in more information and think of more ideas, but hopefully, if you've put in enough work and your unconscious is fully engaged in the problem, an idea will come.

4. Illumination. This is the stage where the idea comes to you. As it bubbles up from your unconscious, it can feel like it's just popped into your mind from nowhere. It will often come to you when you are doing some mundane activity like walking, taking a shower or doing the washing up. These activities give the conscious mind something to focus on. The quieting of that constant mental chatter gives us a chance to hear the thoughts coming from our unconscious. It's like tuning in a radio: suddenly we can hear what the unconscious has to say.

When an idea does pop into your head, make sure that you make a note of it. It can seem amazingly vivid at the time, but ideas can also be very fragile, and if you don't keep a record of them, they can be lost forever.

5. Implementation. Although ideas can come fully formed, more often than not they're a bit rough around the edges and will need work. An idea can seem very clear in your head, but as soon as you try to get it down on paper, it can fall apart. But just because it's hard to get an idea to work, it doesn't mean that it's not a good idea. At the other end of the spectrum, you can think that your idea's the best thing since sliced bread and that it doesn't need any work. But whatever you think of your idea, it's important to get the opinions of people you trust, whether that's friends, family or colleagues.

The world is full of critics, so you've got to make sure that your idea is as strong as it can possibly be. Too many good ideas get destroyed because they're released too early. Imagine that your idea is going to court and you are its defence counsel. You need to see whether there are any flaws in its case before it gets cross-examined in the court of life. If you're successful, you get to execute your idea and make it a reality. If they're successful, they get to execute your idea and chop its head off.

Once you're sure that you've made it as strong as it can possibly be, get it out there. Hopefully, you'll be met by the greatest of compliments: "That's so obvious, why didn't I think of that?"

The Creative Process

Things To Remember

Stage One: Information

• Collect as much relevant information as you can.

• Keep asking why.

• The more time that you spend thinking about the problem, the better your solution will be.

• Be a sponge. Have an open and curious mind and soak everything up.

Stage Two: Imagination

• Think of as many ideas as you can.

• Don't get too attached to your first ideas, just keep thinking.

• Make a note of all of your ideas, even the ones that seem silly. They may spark off another idea later on.

• Keep thinking until you really feel that you can't think of anything else.

Stage Three: Incubation

- Keep the problem at the back of your mind, but don't focus directly on it.

- Don't keep the mind too active or inactive. Keep it gently stimulated.

- Let your unconscious mind do its work.

Stage Four: Illumination

- An idea will pop into your head as if from nowhere.

- Make sure that you make a note of it, in case you forget it later.

Stage Five: Implementation

- An idea won't always be fully formed. Make it as good as it can be.

- Get constructive criticism from supportive friends/ colleagues.

- Keep questioning and testing your idea, to make sure that there are no weaknesses.

- Get your idea out there.

Top Ten Tips For
Being More Creative

Be Curious

An inquisitive nature and a thirst for knowledge will create a much more creative mind.

Keep Questioning

Ask the right questions, ask the wrong questions, just keep asking questions. If you really understand the problem, you'll come up with a better solution.

Don't Get Stressed

Getting stuck and not being able to think of anything is part of the creative process. Don't fill your mind with negative thoughts, just keep thinking and let the problem percolate in your mind. Eventually, your unconscious will reward you.

Take Notes

Always make a note of your ideas as soon as you have them, however silly or half–formed they seem. There's nothing that will eat away at you more than a great forgotten idea.

Sleep on it

Sleep has been scientifically proven to help creativity. Sleeping will give you more energy, and it's also when your unconscious does its best work.

Take a walk

So many great ideas have been born on walks. But remember, they're much more effective as a creative tool if you've done some serious thinking before you go on your walk.

Don't Think, Do

It's easy to put off starting something because you don't think that your idea's good enough, or you're not sure whether you've got the skill to execute it properly. The important thing is to start; you can always finesse it later.

Be Prepared To Fail

If you want to come up with original and surprising ideas, you've got to be prepared to fail. You should see it as a chance to learn. As Edison said when working on the light bulb, "I have not failed, I've just found 10,000 ways that won't work."

Keep An Open Mind

It's important not to rule anything out. Some of the best ideas can seem a stupid initially. Don't let your mind be too judgemental and try not to self-censor ideas.

Get Out Of Your Comfort Zone

It's been scientifically proven that doing things differently makes you more creative. Break your routine and go to different places, talk to different people, read different books and magazines.

References

James Webb Young, *A Technique For Producing Ideas*, McGraw-Hill, 2003.

David Eagleman, *Incognito*, Canongate Books, 2011.

BBC Horizon – "The Creative Brain: How Insight Works"

Daniel Kahneman, *Thinking Fast and Slow*, Penguin Books, 2011.

Elizabeth Gilbert, TED Talk: "You Elusive Genius"

Maria Popova, www.brainpickings.org/

Norman Doidge, *The Brain That Changes Itself*, Penguin Books, 2008.

Matthew and Sandra Blakeslee, *The Body Has A Mind Of its Own*, Random House, 2007.

Ray Kurzweil, *How To Create A Mind*, Penguin Books, 2012.

The Numskulls comic strip, *The Beano*

Acknowledgements

Firstly I'd like to thank all the family and friends whose encouragement, support and advice helped me get this book from first draft to final draft: my brothers, Andrew and James Pavitt, Jane Simmons, Gary Betts, Trevor and Mary Pavitt, Roy Millman, Nigel Ward, Julian Dyer, Ravi Karawdra, Craig Hanratty and with particular thanks to Craig Storti and my mother, Jo Pavitt for reading version after version.

I'd also like to thank everyone who helped turn it from a manuscript into a book: Andrew Rott for all his invaluable advice and help with the cover design, Aldy Akbar for the cover design itself, Liz Broomfield for proofreading the book and correcting all my grammatical errors and Jane Dixon-Smith for turning it into a well designed and properly laid out book.

Finally, I'd like to thank my wonderful wife Kalya, who's been there from the start, who's seen it in all it's various forms and various titles and various covers and overly enthusiastic completion dates and never once uttered the words of my son, "Are you nearly there yet?"

And to Harry – "We're there!" (Although you may not be best pleased when you find out I didn't choose the cover design with the tomato on the front.)

About the Author

For over twenty-five years, Neil Pavitt has been an award-winning writer in the advertising and television industries. He has had a short film nominated for the BAFTA New Writers award and spent a short stint as a stand-up comedian. He now works as a creative consultant and runs talks and workshops helping people to become more creative. To find out more, visit www.thelightbulbidea.com.

6663167R00066

Printed in Great Britain
by Amazon.co.uk, Ltd.,
Marston Gate.